CHAKRAS FOR BEGINNERS

Awaken Internal Energy, Balance Chakras, and Heal Yourself

John Smith

CONTENTS

INTRODUCTION

Just picking up this book, you might be wondering what a chakra is and how it can help you. There is no need to fear, as this book will take you through a step-by-step guide to understanding all the essential chakras and how they affect you. This book is meant for people that are unknown with the concept of chakras or would like to start learning about different aspects of the body in connection with spirituality. This book will give you a basic understanding and extensive explanation of chakra points. The concepts discussed will explain these sacred energy points that balance your body physically and mentally.

This book will cover the different imbalances that can manifest from unaligned chakras and even how to fix them. This guide has been written to help to make sure that you can effectively balance your chakra points out, maintain and also improve your health, and keep your life energy flowing through each chakra point freely. Finally, we will discuss how a chakra-based meditation is performed and can benefit you. There are many books on the workings of the chakras, although, in this book, we have tried to appeal to the Western world, whose awareness of the chakras may need a reasonable explanation. The chakras are those points in the body through which energy flows. If you feel that you are not getting enough out of your life, it may well be that you need to work toward opening up the energy flow through your chakras, as when these are empowered, you will find that life offers much more harmony.

This book is my way of giving something back to society and you, the reader, in particular. Take this opportunity, and you can change your way of life for the better. You will feel happier and fulfilled, and you will find that your light will radiate over others, making them enjoy the experience of having you in their lives.

CHAPTER 1
WHAT ARE CHAKRAS?

The word chakra initially means "wheel," but it is also a metaphor for the sun. Both meanings of the word hold a significance in understanding what they are. In the Yoga Upanishads, chakras were mentioned in a way that made them seem as if they were viewed as a psychic center of your consciousness and body. In the Yoga Sutras of Patanjali (around 200 B.C.), chakras were mentioned again as intellectual centers. The long tradition of chakras and their use in culture shows how deeply rooted these concepts are in society. Until today, chakras are an essential spiritual field which is actively practiced by millions of people worldwide.

Chakras are aligned in an ascending column on the human body. They are the energy points in your body, and the energy needs to be unblocked so that it can move freely throughout each end to maintain health and vitality. With new age practices, each chakra has an adjoining color that goes with it, but they have always served to balance you in different ways.

Chakras have mental functions as well as physical ones. They represent an aspect of your consciousness, have a representative element, as well as different distinguishing characteristics. Chakras have powerful and vital energy that moves through them. This energy is your life energy, which is commonly referred to as *prana* or *chi*. Your life energy moves from one chakra point to the next through pathways which are called *nadis*. Charkas, when healthy, spin circularly, spinning the life energy that goes through them, keeping your body in balance.

The Importance of Chakras

Chakras are vitally important in your everyday life, without you probably even realizing it. While you probably know that some parts of your body are vital to your existence, such as your mind, organs, and senses, you might not have known that chakras accurately capture the essential core elements of human life. This is due to their ability to keep you connected with your mind, body, and spirit. Chakras act as a bridge to allow you to be spiritually whole, as well as physically healthy. When a chakra is blocked with energy that refuses to move through it, you may suffer illness, emotional distress, and even something as severe as depression. Everyone has probably experienced this imbalance at some point in their lives, by a period of emotional distress or only through a health issue. Each chakra, when blocked, will cause different types of problems. This is because each chakra point represents something different to your mental, emotional and physical health. When all of your chakras are open and working correctly, then you will find balance and peace in your life, both internally and externally.

CHAPTER 2
THE SEVEN CHAKRAS

In the same way, the chakras are centers of energy through which all power passes, and if there is a blockage in any of these areas, then illness or lack of wellbeing may be the result. Although you cannot see the chakras, you can be very confident that they are affecting you every day of your life. Unlike in acupuncture where there are many centers of energy, the Hindus believe that there are seven chakras located throughout the body and these will be described to you, so that you can understand a little more about the problems in your life and why you may be experiencing them.

While many people in the Western world are not familiar with chakras, it is something that they should look around and learn how to understand a little bit better. These chakras are so crucial to the whole body, to how good you are going to feel about the things that are going on around you, and about how well you can interact with other people. While you may not recognize the chakras and you may not understand what they mean, you had probably experienced many times in your life when they were not working correctly for your needs.

To better understand what these chakras are all about, it is good to have a definition present. So what is a chakra? A chakra is primarily a center of energy. It is a word that originates from Sanskrit, and it means a wheel, which will show some of its associations to the function and the spinning energy that interacts with the different neurological and physiological systems that are in the body. These are not just some types of energy centers though, they are ones that are found inside of your body, and they are going to be in charge of regulating all of the processes that occur inside. This can include some things from organ function to your emotions and even how well the immune system works.

For the most part, there are seven main chakras, and they are going to be positioned all throughout the body. Some people believe that there are some lesser chakras, but for now, we are going to focus on some of the more familiar ones and how they are going to work in your body.

Each of the chakras is going to work on a different part of the body. For example, the first chakra is going to be in charge of helping you to feel connections with the other people around you while the crown chakra opens you up to some of the things that happen in the spiritual world. All of the chakras are important, and they even work together, even though they may seem to work in such different parts of the body. When one of the chakras is not working correctly, it can start to affect how the other chakras are going to behave as well over time. If you do not take the time to give the chakras the healing that they need, you are going to start noticing that many of the chakras will begin to fail.

Besides, there are several ways that things can go wrong with the chakras. Many times when there are issues, it is because the chakras are closed off and are not able to let in some of the energy that is needed. For example, when the heart chakra is closed off, you may not be able to experience emotions, and you may be seen as cold-hearted to other people. Besides, you may find that the heart chakra, or any of the other chakras, could be too opened, which could result in you feeling too many emotions and always being a wreck from these emotions.

It is essential that you work on keeping the chakras balanced as much as possible. In our modern world, this can seem like something that is almost impossible to work on. You are already overworked, stressed out, and so much more, so how much sense does it make to try to keep the chakras in balanced if everything in your life is already working against you? It does take a little bit of dedication and hard work, but with some commitment and sticking with it, you can make your chakras as healthy as possible.

In this section, you will find a basic overview of what each of the seven chakras is. When going over the seven core chakras, we will briefly explain them to get a basic understanding. Each chakra will be gone over more thoroughly later on in separate chapters, to give you a better grasp of how each chakra is essential and affects you. For now, let us look at the very brief overview. This overview is essential because it will give you some information on the full picture and the influence of chakras on your entire existence. We will discuss the chakra points from bottom to top. Please refer back to the image at the start of this chapter to see a schematic representation of where the chakra points are located.

Root Chakra

Sanskrit: Muladhara

Color: Red

Element: Earth

Symbol: Lotus flower with four petals

This chakra represents your foundation. It collects the energy produced by the earth and nature. The root chakra makes sure that you feel grounded when it is open properly. It also describes the general feeling of openness. It is located at the base of your spine right in the tailbone region, which you will see in the beginning diagram. When blocked, you will experience emotional issues that will manifest in real life situations, such as struggling with financial independence.

Sacral Chakra

Sanskrit: Svadhishthana

Color: Orange

Element: Water

Symbol: Lotus flower with six petals

Located in the lower abdomen (the second chakra from the bottom), right below your navel, this chakra allows you to connect and accept others for who they are. It is also the chakra of pleasure and passion. This chakra, when open, helps you to embrace new experiences and be a person who is not afraid of change. If it turns out that your sacral chakra is blocked in some way, you will experience this in several possible ways. It might feel as if you have too little creativity, experience issues with sexuality, and even have problems with finding pleasure or passion in everyday life.

Solar Plexus Chakra

Sanskrit: Manipura

Color: Yellow

Element: Fire

Symbol: Lotus flower with ten petals

This chakra allows you to be a confident person, giving you control of your own life. It is located in the upper abdomen. Emotional issues that come with this chakra being blocked include issues of self-worth and the repercussions of having poor self-esteem or self-image.

Heart Chakra

Sanskrit: Anahata

Color: Green

Element: Air

Symbol: Lotus flower with twelve petals

This chakra will affect your ability to love, and without it being clear of negative energy, you will have issues with finding inner peace, joy, and even love. You can also experience a hard time opening yourself up to another person. If you ever experienced problems like these, you might have an imbalance in this chakra point.

Throat Chakra

Sanskrit: Vishuddha

Color: Blue

Element: Ether

Symbol: Lotus flower with sixteen petals

This chakra must be open and transparent so that you have a healthy ability to communicate your thoughts and feelings. When the throat chakra is blocked, you might have experienced different types of communication issues, as well as some possible issues with self-expression. You will even find that you have problems with the truth, both accepting and divulging it. This chakra, as the name suggests, is located near the throat.

Third Eye Chakra

Sanskrit: Ajna

Color: Indigo or Dark Blue

Element: Light

Symbol: Lotus flower with two petals

This chakra is located on your forehead, between your eyes and a little up. When open, you will be able to see the bigger picture and have a better focus. However, if this chakra is closed, you might experience problems with your intuition, imagination, and even lack wisdom. It can also cause difficulty in making decisions and thinking clearly. The third eye is closely related to your senses. Often, otherworldly sights are attributed to this chakra point.

Crown Chakra

Sanskrit: Sahasrara

Color: Violet or White

Element: Spirit

Symbol: Lotus flower with one thousand petals

This chakra represents your ability to be connected with a higher power, as well as the rest of the world as a whole. It allows you to be connected spiritually. However, if it is blocked in some way, it can affect the way you feel about both your inner and outer beauty and appearance. It could cause you to experience a lack of spirituality and faith when it is blocked as well. You may even have issues experiencing bliss or peace.

CHAPTER 3
WHY WE SUFFER

One of the primary goals of the original Buddha was to meditate on what caused human suffering. What Siddhartha Gautama found amazed him and it is still very relevant today. He found that humans caused much of the pain that happened within the course of their lifetimes. Thus, he went to work on how to diminish that suffering and came up with the rules that are followed by the people of the Buddhist persuasion. A lot of these are common sense, but we do not think about them enough because we are too busy making mistakes in our lives—the consequences of which are suffering.

Siddhartha Gautama designed the Eightfold Path for an excellent reason. It dictates that you need to live your life in a certain way. People these days do not do that a lot and are too tempted by the trappings of a consumer society. We are told what we are supposed to look like in TV commercials, for instance.

We measure ourselves by society standards, but what we do when we follow this course is to make ourselves unhappy. We are so busy trying to conform to those standards we feel are important that we forget the necessities of a happy life. In fact, the Eightfold Path comes from dissecting the way that people behave based on "Four Noble Truths":

- Suffering exists—We all know this to be true
- Suffering has a cause—Although not so obvious, it is none the less true
- Pain can end—This we also know to be true
- The truth of the path that frees us from suffering

Siddhartha Gautama went further than that and looked into different reasons why people suffer. He put these into categories that are still easy to understand today, and these make up the Eightfold Path. The Eightfold Path consists of the following things:

- *Right Vision*—Seeing the world for what it offers you and understanding the nature of reality
- *Right Emotion*—Being able to let go of bad things and give from the heart
- *Right Speech*—Thus, you do not say things that hurt either you or others
- *Right Action*—Doing the right thing is always going to give you better results than not
- *Right Livelihood*—That means doing a job that is not harmful to anyone
- *Right Effort*—That means putting yourself out to give enough of yourself to the task at hand
- *Right Mindfulness*—This means being aware of the world around you and your relationship with it
- *Right Concentration*—This means putting in the effort and disciplining your mind to continue to concentrate

You can see that if you were to apply all of these to your life, you would live a pretty peaceful existence. They all matter in the way that we react in life. For example, a man who worked in a job that he knew would endanger people would have the problem of conscience. Add to that; he decides to do nothing about it, and he has not taken the right action.

We see people on the TV all the time that know something is wrong, but who carry on regardless, and that does not make them happy. Susan, who joined our class, was someone who knew that she was not always as mindful as she could be. Her problem was that she tended to overthink things, and all of these thoughts would go around in her head so that she never really had time to notice her life was slipping by in a very retrospective manner. She was not doing the things she needed to do because her mind was so filled that it did not have any room left for positive thoughts.

When you look sincerely into the Buddhist philosophy and bear in mind that it is a philosophy rather than a religion, you find that the rules still apply as much today when it comes to human suffering as they did when they were written 5,000 years before Christ! That is pretty amazing. It is hoped that now you understand the rules that make life more comfortable to live, you will be able to take the following chapters seriously and learn how to make these actions and thoughts relevant to your own life. If you are suffering at all, you need to find the source of the suffering.

Too many times, we feel that we need to have more stuff in our lives. We need to be mean to other people to get ahead, we need to work all of the time to make more money, and we need to have somehow more things to be better than everyone else. That is what this materialistic world has taught us to believe as the road to happiness, but it is indeed a world that is going to ruin the chakras and will lead us to feel miserable in no time.

Instead of focusing on all of these materialistic things that do nothing for making us happy and often lead us to feel empty and alone, it is time to look inwards to find that happiness. Learning how to work with your chakras and using some of the methods that are explained in this guidebook for dealing with the chakras is one of the best ways to help you to find that inner peace.

While the world has spent so much time lying to us about what makes us happy, it is helping us to ruin the right chakras that are inside of us all. You may need to find a way to break against all of these thoughts and the popular beliefs in our culture if you ever want the chance to feel happy and fulfilled. It is going to take some time and effort, but with the right mindset and understanding why you are feeling so unhappy and miserable now, it is possible to change things around.

CHAPTER 4
CHAKRAS AND YOU

Your chakras are an integral part of your daily life. While many people do not realize what is going on in their bodies, most of the time your chakras are the parts that control this. When things seem to be wrong in the shape, like you feel overwhelmed or have trouble talking to other people, your chakras may be the reason that you are dealing with this. On the other hand, when you feel perfect about your life, you feel like you can talk to other people, love other people, and you do not feel like things are wrong, your chakras are most likely aligned together.

Knowledge of the chakras and how you can strengthen them is vital to your overall physical, mental and spiritual health. Chakras are typically defined as the (sometimes) invisible force fields around you, which emanate positive or negative energies depending on your mood, emotions and health status.

The chakras are so crucial to your body. Even if just one of the chakras is poorly aligned, you will notice that all of them can become blocked and not working that well. All of the chakras need to have energy flowing through them properly so if one of the chakras does not allow the energy to flow through, there are going to be some significant problems that arise. You need to learn how to let the energy flow through the chakras to help them to feel better, and this can be done in no time at all.

When the chakras are opened up, you will notice that you feel so much better than ever before. Opened chakras allow you to talk to others, open up your heart to others, feel grounded in the world around you, and even to have a connection to a higher power. All of these can be important to live a happy and healthy life. In many cases, our modern world makes it difficult to keep the chakras working as well as you would like them to. We are too stressed out, we are worried about keeping our jobs, and we may not have much of a chance to open up to some other people. It does take some active work to help keep the chakras as open up as possible.

When the chakras are closed up, you will quickly notice that there can be issues that arise as a result of this. You may feel shy when you are with other people. You may not be able to show or share the love with some of the other people in your life, or you may not be able to stay grounded in the life that you have. There are so many elements of your life that can go wrong when you are dealing with your chakras not working correctly and if one of the chakras is out of order, and not letting through the energy that you need, all of them can begin to fail pretty quickly.

Another problem that you may have is that chakra will allow in too much energy compared to what it should. For example, if your throat chakra is open too much, you may blurt out anything that comes into your head, even if it is not necessary or will cause a lot of pain to someone else when you do not need to do this. When the throat chakra is working correctly, you will find that it works well to help you show honesty and speak up correctly, so you do not want it to let in too much and say a lot of things that are not necessary and could cause issues with other people.

Working on the chakras is one of the best things that you can do for your overall health. It allows you to improve your life better than ever before because you get the chance to understand how all of the chakras work together and how they influence the different parts of your life. When you can get them to work together well, you will notice a massive improvement in your life in no time.

CHAPTER 5
BREATHING TECHNIQUES
TO HELP YOUR CHAKRAS
REMAIN OPEN

The way that you breathe every day of your life may be enough to keep you alive, but have you ever examined it to see if you are doing it most effectively? Many people assume that breathing is merely a matter of taking air into the body and then expelling it. What you need to recognize is the different levels of breath and what they do to you. For example, if you get tense easily and find yourself overly stressed, you may just be breathing too quickly. You may know the system that people use to calm down again. They blow into a bag. What this does is to alter the level of carbon dioxide in the blood so that you can calm down. How can you be positive when you are so anxious your breathing is letting you know something is wrong? The fact is that you cannot. This is why you need to learn breathing techniques that help you in different circumstances. The first thing that you need to do is learn to breathe correctly.

The flow of air through your body is essential, but did you know that you can block your chakras if you do not respect your authority? When Ken started his yoga course, he did not do any of this. In fact, he spent so much time, sitting with his back crouched, watching TV that he was not aware of the importance of a straight spine. Just imagine what this kind of habit is doing to your chakras! Learning to sit correctly and breathe the way he was supposed to breathe made a world of difference for him. He said that he learned to respect his body more and that when he breathed correctly, he felt superbly well for the first time in years. "I thought yoga was all about twisting into different difficult positions," he said, "though the obvious thing of breathing was the last thing I thought of as helping to improve my health and wellbeing."

Learning to Breathe Correctly

Without thinking of anything else at all, concentrate on your breathing. Imagine the breath that goes in and out of your body like substantial energy. Hold your head with your chin down and breathe in through the nostrils to the count of seven. Hold the breath within you for a moment and then breathe out through either the mouth or the nose, depending on what is more comfortable for you.

You may think, that is all there is to breathe. If you want to work on freeing up your chakras, there is a little more to it. As you inhale to the count of 7, feel the air enter your upper abdomen. Place your hand there, so that you can contact your abdomen swell, hold the breath and as you breathe out, feel that pivoting motion. Keep doing this until the pivoting movement takes on a rhythm. It is important to do this over and over again. While you are in the practicing stage, try to ignore all the things around you. Try not to slouch and also concentrate entirely on your breathing and the motion of your abdomen.

Alternate Nostril Breathing

This kind of breathing exercise will help you because it calms the mind. It also means that you can let go of the tension. If you find yourself in a situation where you feel out of control, find a quiet spot and practice this type of breathing because it will help align the chakras and you will feel much better for it.

Remember with all breathing exercises that the breathing should not be a forced thing. These are relaxing activities to help you to unwind and should not be considered, in any way, physically. You can also check your abdomen movements while you do alternative nostril breathing because that gives you a clue as to whether you are taking enough air into the right parts of the body. Do not try to do it faster as this has no beneficial effect whatsoever. Take your time. Relax and enjoy the air you breathe. You may even enjoy doing these exercises in a place where the air is fresh, such as at the beach or in the country, but they are equally effective wherever you are. The bonus with the countryside or the beach is that you also have the inspiration of nature all around you. That is when the real magic happens. Absorb it and let it help your chakras to allow energy to pass. You will know when it has happened.

As you saw above, there are a few different methods that you can use when it comes to doing these breathing exercises that will be discussed more in the next chapter. The critical thing to remember is the breathing that you do during these exercises needs to be slow and relaxed. When we go through our daily activities, we are often working a lot harder than we realize. Our breath is going quickly because we are running around for different tasks, feeling stressed out, or even angry about something that is going on in our lives. This can make it hard to calm down, and we may be breathing heavy and fast without even noticing it.

This is why it is so important to find a method that will help you to slow the body down a little bit more. You do not want to keep the breathing going so fast, or you will never be able to help the chakras feel better than before. You can use any method that you want, but the first few minutes of doing meditation or another deep breathing exercise should be focused on just slowing the breathing down and feeling a lot better.

If you find that looking around is not providing you with the results that you would like, you may want to try closing your eyes a little bit. This will make it easier just to shut out all of the things that are bothering you through the day and will make it easier to calm the breathing down. Just some deep inhales to fill up the lungs and then some slow exhales for a few minutes will do some wonders to ensuring that you get the results that you would like.

Deep breathing is so good for your overall health, and when combined with meditation, you will start to notice that it is a fantastic way for you to work on strengthening the chakras and feeling better than before. Even if you are feeling a little bit stressed out and need a few minutes to yourself, you will find that working with some deep breathing for even five minutes will make a big difference.

CHAPTER 6
DOING MEDITATION FOR CHAKRAS

♦ ♦ ♦

Meditation can be useful for the whole body. Whether you are looking to reduce your anger, reduce the amount of stress that you are feeling or to help your body in some other way, working on meditation can help you out so much. Many people who are working on enhancing their chakras will choose to work on reflection to make this happen a bit more. Meditation helps you to focus just on the chakras a little bit, focusing on what is so essential for your overall health.

If you are interested in using meditation to help out with your chakras, there are some critical steps that you can take to make this happen in your life. First, decide if you would like to work on all of the chakras in a session or if you want to focus on one or two. This demonstration is going to look at how to work on all of the chakras in one sitting, so you know how to do it, but you are more than welcome to work on just one at a time if you would like.

So, when you are ready to work on your chakras, follow some of the same instructions from above. You will want to start with finding a beautiful quiet place where you can be all by yourself. If there are a lot of noises around you or other distractions, you are going to have a hard time working on the chakra that you would like. So go to a room that is comfortable and where you can be alone for some time, to get a deep concentration that you need.

Next, make sure that your posture is beautiful and healthy. You want to make sure that the chakras can line up well together when you are working on this part, and if you are slouched over and uncomfortable, this is just not going to happen. The best thing that you can do is to sit up nice and straight, adding in a pillow to your butt if it helps to support you a little bit. If you have some troubles with sitting on the floor, you may want to consider using a chair to sit on, make sure that you are sitting up as straight as possible.

When you are ready, close your eyes and start concentrating on the deep breathing that you need to calm down. Going straight into this from a hard and stressful day can be hard on you and will bring in more challenges in getting things done. So spend a minute or two working on some of the deep breathing exercises that were discussed before and then your heart rate and your concentration will be right where they should be.

At this point, it is time to start concentrating on the chakras. Start with the root chakra and move your way up as you go through this process. Each chakra has a different color, with the first three being the warm colors, the red, orange, and yellow, and the top ones are going to be the cooler colors like green, blue, indigo, and purple. You will be able to use these colors as you move through all of the chakras.

But for now you are just going to concentrate on the root chakra, and nothing else; you can get to the other ones a little bit later. Think about the color red while you are doing your deep breathing. It is probably going to come in as a dull color in the beginning, but you will want to concentrate on giving it some power and making it a bit stronger. As you focus on the chakra and the color red, it is going to become brighter and brighter until they burst out and are as bright as you can handle. When you get to this point, you know that the root chakra has gotten some of the attention that it needs and you can move on to the next chakra.

You will keep going through this process from the root chakra all the way to the crown chakra, allowing each of them to have some time to get beautiful and sharp on their own. You may find that some do not need as much attention as the others so do not feel bad if you take a bit longer on one of them and then the next one is going faster. Each person is going to make their amount of time on the chakras so go at your own pace, do not rush things, and relax while you are getting it all done.

As you can see, going through all of the chakras can be a lot of work for some people, and if you do not have that much time available to get it done, it is okay to work on one or two chakras a day to help keep them healthy. When you are all done with working on the chakras for the day, and you feel like you have given them some of the cleansings that they need, you can slowly get up and out of the meditation, and then go on with the rest of your day, feeling so much better and more fulfilled than ever before.

Doing meditation for your chakras can be a fantastic way to take care of your body and your spirit. While many people spend that time reducing their stress levels and such, many are finding that this is also a fantastic way to work on their chakras. The work for doing this is not that hard, but it does take a little bit of time and effort to get it done. If you can follow some of the techniques that are in this chapter, you are sure to strengthen your chakras and make them feel better than ever.

CHAPTER 7
BALANCING YOUR
CHAKRAS

Balancing your seven chakras is essential because when one of your chakras is not balanced, your emotions and your body might be affected. When you are with someone who is sad or happy, it is highly possible for you to channel these emotions. You become a magnet of energy! However, too much lousy power could weaken your state, and you could feel ill. Be responsible for your own emotions. The information below will guide you as to what happens when there is an imbalance in your feelings: Anger gives you flashes of red. This is such intense energy that emanates from a person—too much of it is terrible for your body as it absorbs other harmful elements. When you are angry, know that there is a chakra imbalance in the solar plexus.

On the other hand, being defensive puts armors or cords around you. Defensiveness signals an imbalance in your brow and solar plexus chakras. Whenever this happens, you feel that you want to alienate yourself from other people. You dislike relationships and reject pieces of advice and help from friends and relatives.

Resentment clouds your vision. Almost similar to anger, bitterness makes you unable to think clearly. Making decisions is also difficult for you. There is an imbalance in the heart and solar plexus. The same thing happens when you are unfortunate. It is like there is a cloud before your eyes. This means there is an imbalance in your heart and crown chakras. Address this quickly. Otherwise, you could feel depressed and anxious.

Jealousy, in contrast, enables hooks of energy to trap you. You feel angry and resentful at the same time. You want to pour your energy into things that are not worth your time — being jealous. You also become possessive of people. Remember that there is an imbalance of the heart, solar plexus and brow plexus. Lastly, hysteria results in fragmentation. You feel disconnected. There will be times when you cannot explain and express what you think. Communication is difficult. Hysteria is the worst form of emotional and auric disturbance; hence, all the chakras are affected.

Bringing Back the Balance to Your Chakras

To rebalance your chakras, first, you have to create a sacred space for yourself. You could use natural elements here; either surround yourself with the features that represent fire, water, wind, and earth; or use your crystals and gemstones to create a sacred circle. Sprinkle salt around the sacred circle to purify it. Next, ground yourself and connect with the energy of the earth. A simple way to do this is to lie on the floor.

Connect with the cosmic energy as well. Imagine that golden energy or a yellow light is surrounding you. This light comes from your crown chakra, passes to your heart chakra region, then to your hands. Imagine this light going down to your toes.

Say an affirmation or a prayer to invite your spirit guide, or to at least welcome the cosmic energy. You could start with the *"I Have the Right"* affirmation. Since the chakras are connected to your body and your emotions, you can say this prayer and mantra.

The next step is to scan the aura thrice. Do this with your dominant hand, as you lie on your back. Start at the top of the head, then use your hand to go over your body down to your feet. Be sensitive to where your chakras are blocked. If you feel any difficulty, use your pendulum to do that for you.

Note on pendulums: Any necklace will do, actually, but it is best to use a crystal dangling from a chain. Use your intuition when choosing a swing.

Open your chakras using your dominant hand. Imagine a golden light coming from your side and use it to go over your body. Spin your dominant hand three times to scan your aura. This will get rid of your blockages. Lastly, the pendulum will guide you to where your energies are blocked. As you hold the pendulum upright, say, "I am now testing the chakra. Is this blocked?"

When the pendulum says that, there are areas that are blocked, use your hand to balance the chakra point. Move your hand on top of the blocked region and imagine the golden light from your hands cleansing the area blockage. After moving your hand across the blocked chakra point, refer to your pendulum to check if the obstruction has been removed.

If the chakra point has been opened, seal the positive energy by spinning the golden light from your hands on that chakra point three times, counterclockwise. Sweep your hand from the top of your head down to your feet to seal the auras. When you are done, cross your arms over your chest and thank your spirit guides.

CHAPTER 8
AWAKENING YOUR
SEVEN CHAKRAS

It is important that you awaken your chakras before you use them for your healing. All people have chakras in their body; these points are not just active. A re-birthing session must take place first before you awaken your chakras. During the re-birthing stage, you have to exhale in a relaxed way. Visualize that the air you breathe is passing through your chakra points.

Root Chakra

To awaken your root chakra, first, stand with your feet wide apart. Make sure that you are comfortable. Next, rotate your hips from right to left. Do this about 48 to 50 times. Breathe deeply as you rotate your hips, and take three directed breaths when you are done. Repeat the same procedure (hip rotation) from left to right. Follow this with three directed breaths.

Navel Center Chakra

Just like in the root chakra, take 49 to 50 re-birthing breaths and then tuck your stomach in sharply. You do not want to harm yourself when you get started with this one, but do draw your stomach back a little bit to help you to work on the navel center chakra. This will make a big difference in how much you will be able to feel this particular chakra.

Heart Chakra

Awaken your heart chakra by stretching your arms sideways. Take 49 re-breathing breaths whole circularly moving your arms. Move your arms up and down, and then take three directed breaths. Repeat the process.

Throat Chakra

Drop your head forward and then do a head roll, first to the left, then to the back, and then forward. As you move your head, breathe deeply. You must be able to have seven re-birthing breaths after each head roll.

Third Eye Chakra

Empower your third eye by taking 49 re-birthing breaths and raising your eyebrows quickly as you open your eyes. After that, close your eyes and concentrate on your breathing.

Crown Chakra

Raise your arms as you take seven directed breaths. Feel the energy and imagine it encircling you from head to foot.

CHAPTER 9
CHAKRAS, ENDOCRINE SYSTEM, AND THE IMMUNE SYSTEM

Chakras and Glands

If you notice the locations of the glands, you will see that they are more or less placed close to different chakras. Although the traditional systems do not speak about the connection between chakras and glands, the modern followers and experts started outlining clear links between the various chakras, glands, organs and the immune system of the body.

Each chakra is connected to different glands of the endocrine system and facilitates the smooth functioning of that particular gland. Here is a list of the various chakras, the organs they regulate, their functions and the signs of warnings associated with an inefficiently functioning gland/chakra.

Root Chakra

This is connected to the adrenal glands and stands for self-preservation and physical energy. The issues that the root chakra and the adrenal glands handle are associated with survival and security. The fight or flight response of the adrenal glands located at the top of the kidneys is directly connected to the survival drive of the root chakra.

A weak root chakra could result in a weakened metabolism and immune system resulting from a compromised working of the adrenal glands that are responsible for releasing and producing chemical messengers needed for all the physiological, chemical and biological functions of your body.

A not-so-strong root chakra results in nervousness and a sense of insecurity whereas an overly working root chakra could result in greed and a sense of excessive materialism.

Sacral Chakra

Governs the reproductive glands which are the ovaries (for the females) and the testes (for the males). The well-balanced and healthy sacral chakra facilitates the uninterrupted functioning of these glands ensuring well-developed sexuality in the person.

The sacral chakra also regulates the production and secretion of the sex hormones. The potential for life formation in the ovaries is reflected in the sacral chakra as these two energies are connected.

When this chakra is open and free, you can express your sexuality well without being overly emotional. You feel a comforting sense of intimacy with your partner. A healthy sacral chakra enhances your passion and liveliness and helps you manage your sexuality without feeling burdened with extreme emotions.

A sacral chakra that is not functioning at its peak efficiency is bound to leave you frigid, very close to people and relationships, and poker-faced. On the contrary, a weak sacral chakra will make you feel overly and unnecessarily, emotionally compelling you to attach yourself to people for a sense of security and belonging. Your feelings could be excessively sexual towards one and all.

Solar Plexus Chakra

This controls the pancreas, which is directly connected to the sugar (through the control of insulin secretion) and, therefore, energy levels in your body. Thus, if this chakra is not working correctly, you could potentially have a weak pancreas, resulting in a compromised metabolic state. Compromised pancreas could lead to digestive problems, lowered blood sugar levels, ulcers, poor memory, etc. which are all connected with a bad metabolism.

Heart Chakra

Regulates the thymus gland and through it, the entire immune system. Being the center of love, compassion, spirituality, and group consciousness, a malfunctioning heart chakra will result in the malfunctioning of the thymus gland leaving you prone to low immunity.

Our feelings and thoughts towards ourselves play a crucial role in keeping our immune system working well. When we love ourselves, our immune system is powerful and strong. When we are uncertain of ourselves, our strengths, and our capabilities, we feel disappointed which drives us to react wrongly to negative things.

All these negativities leave our immune system weak, and we end up holding on to toxins. It is imperative to keep our heart chakra healthy by investing time and energy in self-love so that our immune system is strengthened. An underactive heart chakra makes you feel distant and cold, and an overactive one could result in selfish love in your heart. Be wary of both states and work at keeping your chakra balanced.

Throat Chakra

Controls and regulates the thyroid gland and hence is directly responsible for a healthy metabolism and body temperature. This is the center of communication and plays a vital role in the way you speak, write, or think. An unbalanced throat chakra results in a malfunctioning thyroid resulting in overall poor physical, mental, and emotional health.

Third Eye Chakra

Directly controls the functioning of the pituitary gland or the master gland that controls and regulates other organs and glands in the human body. The pineal gland is many times associated with this chakra too, as we already know that a well-coordinated, combined working of the pineal and the pituitary glands is responsible for keeping our entire body, mind, and spirit well-oiled and working well.

Crown Chakra

This regulates the functioning of the pineal gland, which controls our biological cycle and our circadian rhythm.

The Connection between Glands and Chakras

Even the slightest disturbances in the chakras or our energy centers can result in physical manifestations of issues and problems. When the chakras do not function the corresponding glands and organs efficiently they are associated with are also affected.

Chakras as you already know are the energy centers in our body and have no physiological or physical shape or form. These energy centers influence the way we live in different layers of our lives, including the biological, the physical, the emotional, and the psychic layers.

When any of the energy centers malfunction or become imbalanced, the problems are manifested in a physical, mental, or spiritual form. An underactive or an overactive chakra can cause problems for you. Keeping them balanced is critical for your overall health.

Any disturbance even in one energy center could result in problems in any other chakra and related glands and organs.

Glands and Chakra Healing

Chakra healing will lead to improved functioning of the endocrine system that is excellent for physical healing of your body. The connection between organs and chakras represent a link between the energy points in your body to the physiological and bodily functions.

Another useful entry point for chakra healing is the nervous system that is connected to glands and organs in multiple ways and at various locations. A chakra healing session is ideally begun by calming the nerves and then targeting a particular gland and chakra.

By understanding the connection between chakras and the glands, you can use healing in different ways that will help you overcome physical, emotional, mental, and spiritual issues in your body and mind. Connecting the chakras and the glands will help in your overall well-being.

CHAPTER 10
EXERCISES FOR
PARTICULAR CHAKRAS

The main reason that you need to unblock blocked energy is so that you feel well, and that means emotionally as well as physically. In this chapter, we explore exercises that will help you to handle healing reasonably quickly. These exercises should be done as and when you feel that you need them. Do not think of them in the ordinary sense as you would with practice in general because these are to be done slowly. You do not get extra brownie points for speed. What you are trying to do is unblock those chakras, and they may have been blocked for a very long time. Thus, do not expect instant results. You will start to heal reasonably rapidly, and you will feel a difference, but you need to consistently do the exercises that relate to the chakra that is giving you problems. A word of warning: breathing at the right moment during yoga exercises helps to provide you with more strength. If you do not have an instructor, try to watch videos that give you specific instructions about when to breathe in and when to breathe out.

Root Chakra Exercises

The exercises needed to help you with this chakra are easy to do. Take off your shoes and socks and get ready to stamp your feet on the ground. As you do so, be aware that the whole foot should touch the ground. This chakra relates to that feeling of being grounded. The exercises should be performed several times or over a five-minute period before relaxing with your feet flat on the floor. You will also find a guide to the foods that you should be eating in the next chapter of the book. If you have yoga lessons, ask your teacher to introduce you to the bridge pose, as this is particularly good for the root chakra. This is where your body is supported by the balls of your feet and your flat hands. You may need supervision the first time that you try this or can work using a video, which will give you a good idea of how the exercise should be performed.

Remember that the root chakra is essential for helping you to feel grounded in the world. You will want to make sure that you can feel like you belong in the physical world, without feeling so attached to it that you forget all that is going on around you. It is not a good idea to focus too much on the material things that are going on in your life because these are going to leave you feeling lost and confused because the chakra is going to start failing.

This is why spending some time out in nature and just feeling the earth beneath your feet is so vital for helping you to feel high and full. You will be able to touch the ground and learn what matters, while hopefully being able to let go of some of the materialistic things that are going on in the world around you. Try to save a few minutes each week at least, although doing it each day is the best option, and work on being outside, touching the grass, and even walking around in your backyard to help make the root chakra feel better.

Sacral Chakra Exercises

Several exercises can help you with this chakra. One is an exercise that you have already done. Breathing and moving the abdominal area in rhythm will help this chakra. Pelvic thrusts are the best movements to help open this chakra. These will help to free up the chakra and in turn, help you to heal.

Solar Plexus Chakra Exercises

You may have trouble believing this exercise works, but it does. Dance and get your hips swinging. I told this to one lady who came to me for help and not only did it help her with her self-esteem issues, but she also started to take a course so that she could teach people the same dancing methods. She lost weight; she gained confidence, and at the same time, her chakra healing helped her to enjoy her life to the fullest. This is the most natural form of exercise for people, even for those with little or no experience with yoga. Use Zumba videos from places like YouTube and let it all hang out. As far as yoga exercises are concerned, the ideal training for this region of the body is the boat pose. Lie flat on the floor and then lift your body with your arms stretched forward at the same time as lifting your legs.

Heart Chakra Exercises

This is a critical chakra and one that can make a difference to your happiness in life. Therefore, the activities here are advised for everyone. You can never have too much love in your heart! The best exercise you can use to heal this chakra is to be more aware of others, to learn empathy and to learn humility. When you can open up your heart to others, you will find that you gain a great sense of wellbeing. Be honest and loving and have a smile for people, even when they do not particularly merit it. It is healing for the heart, and it helps you to move past periods of negativity. If you are looking for a yoga style that will help the heart chakra, then the ideal is hot yoga (otherwise known as Bikram Yoga).

Throat Chakra Exercises

The best exercise for this region and one that gives instant relief is head rolling. Sit with your spine straight and look to the right, move your head back and rotate it in an anti-clockwise motion. Do this slowly and surely rather than rushing at it and then do the same thing in the other direction. You will also get great relief for this chakra by allowing yourself the pleasure of singing. It helps to open up the chakra and at the same time can bring you peace of mind.

Third Eye and Crown Chakra Exercises

The exercise of meditation will help both of these, as will breathing exercises that we have already explained. These areas do need your help, and the reason that people do meditation on a daily basis is that the more you do it, the better you get at it, and that helps you to feel very contented in your life. It also helps to relieve all the knotted up thoughts that you may have been gathering in your mind over a period.

I try to explain how the mind works in simple terms to students because they seem to understand it better. Imagine that the conscious mind—or the part of the brain that thinks—is so busy that it has millions of thoughts all piled up one on top of the other. They may be sorted into compartments such as emotional issues, practical issues, responsibilities, obligations, etc. But when you over-use the mind in this way, what you do is break down all the compartments so that they flow into each other. If you can imagine a room full of boxes that have all been opened. The content of these boxes is strewn around the room, and it is a real mess. That is what happens when thoughts too invade your mind.

Now, look at what the subconscious mind does. This part of the memory records everything that happens in your life. It is a logical part of the brain that is seldom accessed. In fact, during REM sleep you may find that this part of the brain can come up with solutions to problems. People who lack sleep will not have the ability to access help from the subconscious mind. However, when you meditate and switch the conscious mind to mundane tasks, you are disciplining it to stop thinking so much or teaching it only to think about the things that you are allowing it to think about. Of course, when thoughts pop into your head, during meditation, you acknowledge them without judgment and then dismiss them because they are not part of the meditation process. By doing that, you are not reacting to the thought, and thus your subconscious can record that you did not react in an adverse way to the trigger that presented itself.

Your subconscious mind is a lot more powerful than your conscious mind. When you meditate, you give yourself access to it and can often gain a greater sense of clarity because of your meditation. The Buddhist monks are trying to reach that inner wisdom that they call Nirvana or "all knowing" and you begin to see the effects of reaching that higher intelligence after you have been practicing meditation for a while. It helps these chakras to heal, and it also means that you will sense a change in your attitude toward life that is more in keeping with harmony and happiness. That is what meditation is all about.

CHAPTER 11
SPIRITUAL AWAKENING

◆ ◆ ◆

The chakras that you have from your throat up to the top of the head are special ones. Whenever you have profound emotional experiences, these chakras get the best treatment that they can because these experiences help you to feel relaxed and happy. Imagine what you feel like when you see a baby smile. It gives you a sense of happiness. Imagine what you think when you get the feeling that your God is with you and giving you strength through hard times. That is the same kind of sense, and these chakras pick up on your happiness level and your level of understanding life in general. People who have activated the third eye say that they can see things from another perspective, and it opens up their level of spiritual understanding. Even if you cannot open up the third eye, the fact that you are willing to take up meditation and exercises to heal your chakras is going to lead to a better understanding of life in general, and that is enlightening.

Let me relate a story of finding that enlightenment myself. I remember being on a package tour to a retreat in Tibet. I was fortunate enough to have the opportunity of being taught "all about spiritual things" by a guru. There we were, surrounded by our suitcases, looking for a hotel atmosphere because that is what most of us thought we would get. I did not mind at all because I had read about retreats such as this and had an idea of what to expect. Others, who came from backgrounds of excess, were a little startled by the difference between this accommodation and their usual accommodations.

We all went through the same classes, though there were those who gained nothing. Others gained something they would never have experienced without learning about meditation and mindfulness. I am not joking. When you do things that you are asked to do or that are expected to do with an open and ready heart, you begin to take note of the tasks and take pleasure in them. No work is too menial because you have learned humility. No goal is too large—because you have learned through meditation that all things are possible.

Take yourself close to nature regularly. It is essential for your peace of mind, and it is also crucial to help you realize how humble you are. That is important because while you have self-importance as the center of your universe, you can never feel that closeness or spirituality that every human being is capable of achieving. Your meditation will help you to find that feeling of joy, and the chakras from the throat upward will celebrate with you when you can use all of your senses, instead of letting them be drowned out by modern society. How often do you listen to the birds singing in the morning? How often do you see a sunset and enjoy it? How often do you taste a piece of fruit and let the taste linger so that your tongue and mouth get the full sensation? All of these joys are available to those who are mindful enough to make the most of their senses. In fact, blind people compensate for the loss of sight by using alternative senses and are often much more spiritual because of this adaptation.

Spiritual awakening is what makes the chakras open to the regular flow of energy. Each time that you breathe in the fresh air or place your fingers in a pile of snow, you open up senses that you have perhaps neglected in favor of modern life. The child within you needs to experience these things. Your sense of touch will give you many pleasures, and your sense of hearing can also do this. The taste will always make you feel good if you choose the foods you eat for their flavor rather than because they are cheap and fast to eat. Stop and enjoy.

Your crown chakra is opened up to the sensation of fresh air when you walk away from the city or find a place where you can be reminded of the natural elements of the world. If you live in a town, take time out, visit the park at lunchtime and sit, and eat your lunch without rushing.

Be mindful of people around you and of the way that you interact with them. If you go back through the chapters of this book and can walk the Eightfold Path; you do not have Buddhist! You can be of any religion or none at all. It is the common sense route to stopping the pain in your life and making your life a much more worthwhile place to be.

CHAPTER 12
PROBLEMS THAT SOME
OF THE CHAKRAS MAY
ENCOUNTER

There are times, though, when your chakras may be blocked or imbalanced. This often happens because of emotional upset, caused by either accident, conflicts, or any form of loss. There are also times when you get overly stressed and anxious and, in turn, your chakras suffer. Here are some of the issues that could lead to blockage of the chakras.

Root Chakra

The root chakra suffers when you feel like you cannot protect or cover your basic needs, or when you feel like you cannot put your necessities in order. When this happens, you get to feel like your prostates are affected, and feel problems in your feet, legs, male reproductive parts, and the immune system. These could then lead to eating disorders, sciatica, knee pain, and even degenerative arthritis.

To get this back in balance, you have to start believing that you have the right to be on earth and that you have an essential role to play. Once you get this back in balance, you would feel grounded, supported and connected to the world.

Sacral Chakra

The sacral chakra is affected when you cannot express your emotions well, and when you cannot stay committed.

These then cause urinary problems, sexual and reproductive issues, low back and pelvic pain.

To get this back in balance, you should allow yourself to take risks, stay committed and creative. You also have to learn to be passionate, outgoing and positively sexual. Once that is done, you will easily be able to honor others—and yourself.

Solar Plexus Chakra

When your self-esteem is low, and when you feel like you cannot believe in yourself, your solar plexus chakra suffers. It also hurts when you fear criticism because of being criticized too much in the past, or when you do not feel good about your physical appearance.

When that happens, you may experience digestive problems, high blood pressure, liver dysfunction and problems in the colon and intestines.

To get this back in balance, you have to make sure that you accept yourself—no matter who or what you are; or what you can and cannot do. When that happens, you will be able to have more self-respect and compassion, and you will be more confident and assertive.

Heart Chakra

When you love people to the point of suffocation, your heart chakra suffers. It also hurts when you become overly jealous, bitter, and angry or when you abandon others without notice. This then leads to heart diseases, asthma, lymphatic system problems, breast cancer, shoulder and upper arm problems, as well as wrist pain.

You should then get the heart chakra back in balance by always letting joy, compassion, and gratitude rule over your life. You should also learn to let forgiveness flow and learn to give trust, as well.

When that happens, you would learn how to love— whether yourself or also the people around you.

Throat Chakra

The throat chakra gets to be blocked when you cannot speak or write about your thoughts clearly, and when you feel like others are dictating what you have to do for you. In short, you would get to feel as if you do not have any choices at all. This could then lead to a sore throat, thyroid issues, facial problems, ulcers and ear infections, together with neck and shoulder pain.

To get this back in order, you have to make sure that you let your voice be heard and that you speak your mind. When this happens, you will be able to be honest and firm, expressive, communicative, and also be a good listener.

Third Eye Chakra

The third eye chakra is said to be the most complicated, and not the easiest one opened. When you get too moody or let your emotions cloud your judgment, this chakra is affected. This is also changed when you daydream too much and let your imagination burn reality down. More than that, it is blocked when you forget to reflect on the state of your life, and when you become volatile—in whichever way possible.

To stop the blockage, you should learn to look at the big picture instead of overanalyzing things. Once this happens, you will be able to have some clarity; you would be able to focus on things that need your attention, be able to recognize fears and not let them take over your life and get to learn from others, as well. This way, you would gain more insight and wisdom and get to appreciate life more.

Crown Chakra

Finally, you have to understand your crown chakra. This gets blocked when you always try to find greater power than you have, and when you have problems using your knowledge and skills efficiently. Sometimes, it also gets affected when you let political and religious difficulties bother you too much when you carry prejudices against others when you over-analyze, and when you are scared of being alienated or being alone.

Now that you know what blocks each of the chakras, you should now be able to live your life in such a way that you will not overthink—and that you will always let peace and harmony reign in your life!

CHAPTER 13
HEALING THE CHAKRAS

The traumas and memories of the past leave their imprint on the chakras, and the chakra shuts down, getting blocked completely. It is as if the chakra throws up a defense shield or protective barrier around itself to prevent further injury—like a hard, impenetrable shell.

That defense shield can be tough to break through. If you have experienced trauma connected to the root chakra, for example, it will be too frightening to jump into activities that cause your survival instinct to kick in. You run the danger instead of shutting down and reliving the trauma, which could only serve to harden the protective shell around that chakra.

In that case, it is better to take an easy-going tack and work towards healing the chakra slowly. Treating the wounded chakras involves soothing them, progressively loosening that hard shell until it slowly begins to yield and become pliable.

Figuring Out the Problem

The first thing you will want to do when healing the chakras is to identify on which chakra or chakras that you need to work. That means you have to think about your problem.

It is not always clear which problem has to do with which chakra. For example, say you have crippling shyness and social anxiety. It has reached an extreme point where it is interfering with your life—your social life, no doubt, maybe also your career. To which chakra does that correspond?

First, consider the context. When does it come up? If you start to panic and get tense inside when it comes to talking to someone of the opposite sex (or anyone you might be sexually interested in), then the problem is probably connected with your sacral chakra, which governs sexuality.

Or maybe you have been giving your time and energy to your work, creating value for your company. But it freaks you out too much to ask your boss for a raise that you desperately deserve. Then the problem has to do with assertion and willpower—connected to the navel chakra.

Maybe you do not feel confident to express yourself adequately. You want to communicate but cannot find the right words. Then the problem might have to do with the throat chakra.

Also, notice what kinds of thoughts you have when your problem comes up. Do you get preoccupied with fear about your money situation, or start to panic when you think about finances? You might want to work on healing your root chakra.

When you are getting close to someone emotionally, do you start to have doubts and suspicions about them? If you are as objective as possible, are those doubts rooted in reality? If you are very suspicious and mistrustful of the people close to you for no reason, then you will want to consider healing work on the heart chakra.

Notice emotions and feelings that come up as well. How do you feel when someone close to you shows their love or affection? Do you feel the same emotions in your own heart? Do you feel afraid or uncomfortable? Or apathetic? If something feels off, you will want to work on your heart chakra.

How do you feel when the topic of spirituality comes up? Maybe you have your own spiritual beliefs sorted out. But perhaps not. Do you feel cynical or angry when people express a religious point of view? Or maybe uncomfortable? Do you feel a compulsion to change other people's beliefs when they are different from yours? These could be signs that the crown chakra needs work.

Pay attention to where emotions register in your body. When your problem comes up, you probably feel a rush of energy somewhere in your body. It could be a sinking feeling in your gut. Maybe it is a lump in your throat. Or it could be a feeling in the area of your heart. Wherever the energy is active in your body, these physiological sensations are clues about which chakra is in play.

Those are some preliminary steps you will want to take to diagnose the problem. In general, it is always a good idea to keep 10-20% percent of your awareness of your thoughts, feelings, and physiological sensations. Just be aware of anything that is happening in your body or mind. That will help you do some fine-tuning and make on-the-fly adjustments wherever appropriate.

A Meditation to Heal the Wounded Chakras

Relax your body completely, starting with the muscles in your head and face, moving down to your neck, shoulders, then your arms. Then relax your upper back and chest. Following that, your lower back and abdomen. Then progressively rest your groin, legs, and feet.

Breathing slowly, place your attention on the breath. Count from 1 to 7, resting your mind on the breath and out breath each time. When you reach 7, start again at 1. Do this several times, until your mind relaxes into an expansive and meditative state.

You might have some other meditation technique for getting into that meditative zone of restfulness and healing. If you prefer to use it at this point, that is no problem. The idea is to make your awareness expansive and meditative. So use whatever works for you.

Now bring to mind the wound that pains you—whatever emotional wound it is you need to heal. Do not dwell on it or think about it so much, like picking at a scab with your mind. Get a sense of what it is like and how it feels, without accepting or rejecting it as good or bad.

Once you have allowed yourself to feel your pain directly, without judgment, turn your attention to the manifestation of energy in the body: Where in the body do you feel any sensations connected with the emotion? Is the power moving or staying in one place? Is it warm or cold? Tense? What other felt qualities does it have?

Feeling the energy in the body can help you locate the chakra you need to heal, as well as any peripheral areas connected to that wound. Try to feel, physiologically and energetically, the knot, tension, or defensive shell that has built up around the chakra. Probe it gently with your mind, to get a sense of how hard or soft it is, firm or yielding, and so on.

Envision your higher power in the space above you. If you are religious, you may want to envision a figure from your religion. You can envision your holy guardian angel or someone else.

From your higher power comes a beam of light that touches your wounded chakra. The color of the fire is the same as the color of the chakra. If you are healing your heart chakra, the sun will be green. If it is the sacral chakra, the light will be orange, and so on.

Imagine the light slowly penetrating the chakra. If the energy of the chakra is hot, the sun will have a refreshing cooling effect. If the power of the chakra is cold, the light gently warms it. Slowly it begins to dissolve the shell surrounding the chakra. Slowly it melts the energetic knots that bind and stifle the energy of that chakra. It also gently heals any wounds and melts away the physical and emotional pain.

Here are some other meditation techniques for some specific chakras.

Root Chakras

Sit comfortably with your legs crossed on the floor or in a chair. Make sure the spine straight, the chest open, and the shoulders relaxed.

Rest your hands on your knees with the palms facing up. Relax your body. Rest the tongue at the top of the mouth, behind the front teeth. Lightly close your eyes.

Breathe deeply down into the low belly, all the way down to the perineum. Aware of the root chakra located between the coccyx and pubic bone. Notice any sensations. Inhale and contract the muscles between the pubic bone and tailbone. Keep your focus on the root chakra as the breath flows in and the muscles contract. Feel the spine lengthen up as the feet and legs ground down. Hold the breath in for 1-2 seconds. Then release and exhale through the nose. Repeat for 3-5 minutes.

Return to a slow deep breath with awareness of root chakra without contracting the muscles. Feel any sensations. Notice any changes. Breathe deeply for 3-5 minutes.

Let the eyes blink open. Inhale and put the palms together in front of the heart, exhale and gently bow. Take a moment and move on to the rest of your day.

Heart Chakra

Sit comfortably with your legs crossed on the floor or in a chair. Make sure the spine straight, the chest open, and the shoulders relaxed.

Breathe slowly into the belly and the chest. Lightly close your eyes. Let go of any thoughts or distractions and focus on breathing. Gently press the knuckles of the thumbs into the sternum at the level of your heart and feel the heartbeat. Keep this for 1 – 5 minutes.

Release your hands. Rub the palms together to make them very warm and energized. Put the right palm in the center of your chest, and the left over the right.

Inhale your arms up towards the sky, connecting with the heavens. Exhale your arms down towards the ground, connecting with the earth. Take a moment and move on to the rest of your day.

Third Eye Chakra

Sit comfortably, either cross-legged on the floor or in a chair with the spine straight, the chest open, and the shoulders relaxed.

Rest your hands on your knees with the palms facing up. Lightly touch the index finger and the thumb. Relax your body. Rest the tongue at the top of the mouth, behind the front teeth. Gently close your eyes.

Breathe slowly and deeply through the nose. With closed eyes, look up at the third eye between the eyebrows. Focus your gaze and concentrate intently on this spot, looking for a white or indigo blue light to appear. Let go of any thoughts that arise in your mind and return your focus to the third eye. Practice this for 10-20 minutes

Inhale your palms together in front of the heart, exhale and gently bow. Gently let the eyes blink open. Take a moment and move on to the rest of your day.

Visualization

Visualization is another excellent technique that you can try out to work on the chakras. We talked about a version of display earlier on when we talked about doing meditation while thinking about the different colors of the chakras, but that is just one of the many ways that you can work on visualization. For those who are having some issues with working on meditation or who need to have something to work on while they are doing the deep breathing exercises, visualization is the choice that you should go with.

When it comes to working with visualization, you are going to spend about ten or fifteen minutes each day focusing on a picture of your choice. You will have some freedom to choose the image that you want to focus on, but you do need to make sure that the movie is of something that is relaxing to you and it is something that you can add in quite a bit of detail about.

With this exercise, we are going to imagine what it feels like to be on the beach. This is a popular choice for many people when it comes to visualization because a beach is seen as relaxing and can help to calm them down at the end of a hard day. To get started with this exercise, you will want to find a quiet place where you can be all alone for a little bit, just like you did when working on meditation.

When you are ready, close your eyes and spend some time taking in a few deep breaths. You want to make sure that the heart rate is pretty steady and ready to go before you go into this activity, or you may rush through it. You can also consider setting a timer for the fifteen minutes if you need to get somewhere, so you do not have to worry about watching the clock.

Once the breathing as slowed down a little bit and you feel comfortable, it is time to work on the visualization a bit. Imagine that you are on the beach on a beautiful warm summer day. Take a look around you and imagine what is all around. Some people may see the beach as empty so that they get the whole place to themselves while others will see other kids and families wandering around and enjoying the day as well. Who is there with you? What are some of the sights and the smells that you encounter? Where would be the best place for you to set up camp so that you can relax?

While you are on the beach, you will want to make sure that you are touching things and getting some of the sensations as well. How does the hot sand feel on your feet and in your hands as you play with it? How do the seashells sound as you pick them up off the ground? Does the cold water of the ocean feel right, or how about that cool, sweet drink when you are trying to relax?

There are so many things that you can imagine when you think about the beach scene, and you are going to want to take your time to go through it as much as possible. Experience that beach scene and enjoy it as much as possible in that time frame. There is no hurry, and there is no limit on what you can experience. If you spend the whole time watching the waves and feeling the cool water lap against your toes, that is just fine. You imagine things in a nice slow pace during that time frame.

When the time is up, you will do a few more slow breaths before heading back to whatever you needed to get done with during the day. You can come back to this scene each day, exploring the things that you liked the most or trying out something new each day to have some fun. You can also change out the scenes that you would want to work with, maybe switching it out with spending time with your kids or having the time to work on your chakras. The choice is up to you but giving yourself some of this time each day to relax and to enjoy the sights and sounds that you would like can help to align the chakras and will ensure that your stress levels are going down as well.

Yoga

Yoga is often one of the preferred methods for helping you to align your chakras. This is often practiced in many of the spiritual schools of thought and the religions that recognize the chakras and can be, as well as being an excellent stretch for the whole body. You have a lot of freedom with the type of yoga that you do. While some poses seem to work the best for specific chakras, there is also a lot of variety, and you can pick out the poses that work the best for you. If you are a beginner with yoga, keep in mind that you can make modifications to the moves and then increase the intensity as you get a bit stronger. You can find some of the steps that you would like to use online or stick with a guided program to help you learn how to do things the right way.

Kundalini Yoga is the yoga for chakras. Its primary purpose is to awaken the Kundalini energy from the base of the spine to the crown of the head. This process begins at the bottom of our spines then travels up the spine, activates each of the chakras along the way. When Kundalini energy reaches the crown chakra, the circuit is complete, and we achieve the Enlightenment. When introduced to the West, it blends the technical and spiritual aspects of yoga to balance and heal ourselves.

Kundalini Yoga combines breath, meditation, and postures to bring harmony to the chakra system. Kundalini Yoga uses poses and pranayama to bring balance to the physical body, introduces the use of voice (chanting) to affect subtle positive changes in the body.

Root Chakra: Since the first chakra is at the base of our spines, poses that help us ground and stand to stimulate this chakra.

- Warrior Pose
- Mountain Pose

- Tree Pose
- Side Angle and Triangle
- Standing Forward Bend
- Bridge Pose

Other poses:

- Child's Pose
- Forward Bend Pose
- Head to Knee Pose
- Warrior II Pose
- Chair Pose

Sacral Chakra: This chakra is the gate chakra for all chakras, and it makes us human, from tears to blood and urination to menstruation. Stimulate this zone with poses that open the hips.

- Bound Angle Pose
- Pigeon Pose
- Cobra Pose
- Child's Pose

Other poses:

- Standing or Seated Wide Forward Bend Pose
- Twisting Triangle Pose
- Sphinx Pose
- Boat Pose

Solar Plexus Chakra: Foster positive energy for personal transformation and keep your belly's fire at a controlled burn.

- Boat Pose
- Sun Salutation
- Bow Pose
- Warrior Pose

- Mountain Pose

Other poses:

- Backbend Pose
- Locust Pose
- Reclining Hero Pose
- Upward Boat
- Half Circle Pose

Heart Chakra: Promote peace and harmony between your physical and spiritual worlds with these poses and other classic back-bending heart openers.

- Camel Pose
- Backbends
- Eagle Pose
- Bridge Pose
- Fish Pose
- Cobra Pose

Other poses:

- Bow Pose
- Cow Pose
- Upward Facing Dog Pose
- Wheel Pose
- Standing Yoga Mudra Pose
- Standing Backbend Pose

Throat Chakra: Purify your being and keep your emotional self-balanced with these poses.

- Fish Pose
- Shoulder Stand Pose
- Camel Pose
- Plow Pose
- Bridge Pose

Other poses:

- Lion Pose
- Half Shoulder Stand
- Rabbit Pose
- Warrior Seal Pose
- Cat Stretch Pose

Third Eye Chakra: Bolster healthy energy flow through the Third Eye with these poses:

- Child's Pose
- Seated Meditation
- Seated Cross-legged / Lotus Pose

Other poses:

- Yoga Nidra
- Corpse Pose
- Easy Pose
- Headstand Pose

Crown Chakra: Although seated meditation is considered the best exercise for this chakra, promote energy center balance with these poses:

- Headstands
- Corpse Pose
- Half Lotus Pose

Other poses:

- Mountain Pose
- Easy Pose
- Seated Yoga Mudra Pose

Gemstones

Some people choose to work with gems to help their chakras to work correctly. The idea with this one is that you will need to pick out the gemstone that is right for the chakra you want to heal. So if you would like to work with the heart chakra you would use a green gem and then if you would like to work on the crown chakra, you would need violet and so on. This can be effective for healing the chakras as long as you use the right colors.

Root Chakra

Stones: Black Tourmaline, Bloodstone, Tiger's Eye, Hematite, Fire Agate, Red Jasper, Ruby

Black Tourmaline is one of the top protective stones.

- Place this stone near your electronic devices, in your house or workplace
- Wear it to absorb negativity and transmute it to positivity energy
- Write your intentions on a small paper and put it underneath this stone

Do This: Place a red crystal between your thighs near the groin and think of the color red — warmth, your foundation, core, family, or your passion.

Sacral Chakra

Stones: Citrine, Carnelian, Moonstone, Coral, Orange Aventurine, Orange Calcite, and Tangerine Quartz

Citrine is one of the beautiful stone for this chakra. Keeping this stone around you keeps you motivated, inspired and confident.

Do This: Place an orange healing stone above the pelvic bone, think of the color orange, and think of yourself as a creative being.

Solar Plexus Chakra

Stones: Malachite, Calcite, Citrine, Topaz, Amber

Citrine, known as the "Merchant's stone," can help you invite prosperity into your life, remove financial blockages, and attract new opportunities.

- Wear citrine stone or keep it in your purse or wallet
- Place it in your cash drawer or money box

Do This: Place a yellow crystal two inches above your belly button, think of the color yellow or a sunny day, and think of your power center and your ability to manifest.

Heart Chakra

Stones: For green: Rose Quartz, Jade, Green Calcite, Green Tourmaline, Malachite, Green Moss Agate, Emerald, Aventurine; for pink: Ruby, Rhodochrosite, and Pink Tourmaline; or for pink and green: Watermelon Tourmaline

Rose Quartz is one of the best gems for relationship troubles and emotional traumas.

- Wear it or hold it when you have emotional problems
- Place it in your home or workplace to keep the atmosphere harmonious and peaceful

Do This: Place a green or pink healing stone on your breastbone, think of the colors pink and green, and think of soothing, mending, opening your heart. Let go of anger.

Throat Chakra

Stones: Lapis Lazuli, Turquoise, Aquamarine, Sodalite, Blue Sapphire

Do This: Place a blue crystal on the larynx, think of the color blue, and think of clear communication, positive speech, and power in your words.

Third Eye Chakra

Stones: Amethyst, Purple Fluorite, Black Obsidian, Iolite

Amethyst is one of the best stone for this chakra. It helps to relieve stress and anxiety, insomnia, and mood swings, and provide extra protection while you are traveling.

Do This: Place a purple stone between the brows, think of the color purple, and focus on your intuition and clarity.

Crown chakra

Stones: Selenite, Clear Quartz, Amethyst, Diamond

Do This: Place a clear or violet crystal above your head, think of bright light, and think of your connection with the divine, God, and spirit.

How do they work?

Laying gemstones on the body for healing has been practiced across for thousands of years. But how? Think about a quartz watch. When quartz crystal is bent, it puts out a constant voltage that keeps a watch running with phenomenal accuracy. Gemstones do the same for us. They interact with our biomagnetic field and create more harmony and balance.

Every stone has a unique vibration. Gemstones for healing will vary from person to others. That is why many books have different suggestions.

How to choose the right gemstones

Look for the gemstones that attract you with their glow.

Feel the energy with your hands. If it is a warm or tingling sensation, that is the stone for you.

How to cleanse and charge gemstones

Do not forget to cleanse your healing crystals and stones before and after you use them.

Sea Salt

- Mix a tablespoon of salt in a glass or ceramic (plastic or metal) cup of cold water.
- Place the stones in the solution and soak overnight.

For dry salt: Place the sea salt in a glass and bury the crystals with the points facing downward into the salt. Leave overnight.

Moonlight

Place gemstones outside from the full moon to the new moon to clear crystals and dispel old energies. Waning moons are good times but anytime the moon is visible will work.

You can hang the gemstone necklaces in a tree where the moonlight can cleanse them.

Herbal

Burying crystals in a cupful of dried herbs (rose petals, sage, frankincense, myrrh, and sandalwood) will clear them.

It is a gentle way, but it takes longer than the sea salt method.

Earth

Dig a hole the size of the crystal into the earth, place the crystal point down, and cover with soil overnight.

You may use a flower pot to bury stones.

Smoke

Hold the burning cedar or sage stick while passing the stone through the smoke couple times back and forth.

Cool water

Run crystals under fresh tap water with the points are facing down.

Use: bottled water, rainwater or boiled water or natural water from a spring, creek or river

Do not use: warm or hot water or standing waters, such as a pond, lake or marsh

Sunlight

Put the gemstones on a clean and soft surface and leave them in the sunlight through the day.

More tips

Sleep with a chakra bag

Clean your stones and place them in a small bag that is only used to hold your stones. Place the bag under your pillow.

Ask the stones to balance you as you are sleeping before you go to bed.

Carry your crystals with you

You can carry your stones with you.

Place them as close to your body as possible.

For example, if you have relationship problems, you can carry a rose quartz stone with you to balance your heart chakra.

Healing the Chakras with Herbs

For millennia, the medical science of Ayurveda has been practiced in India as a way of improving the body and promoting a holistic, preventive approach to the health of body and mind. Ayurveda is concerned in part with the energy in the body and is an excellent supplement to practices that work with the chakras and the subtle energy system.

Many herbs resonate with the energy of particular chakras and can be used to heal and balance them. I will give a few choices for each chakra because some of these herbs might be hard to find where you live. That goes especially for the

Ayurvedic medicines, which may not be readily available in stores.

Herbs for the Root Chakra

Ayurveda: A tremendous ayurvedic herb for remedying problems with the root chakra is shilajit. Shilajit is a pretty weird supplement, but it is mighty and beneficial. It is a dark brown or black, tarry substance that oozes from between the rocks in the high Himalayas.

As the Indian tectonic plate has pushed up against the Eurasian plate, it has caused the earth to buckle, raising up the vast Himalayan mountain range. Over long centuries, it has transformed into the potent tarry substance shilajit.

Shilajit is full of minerals, vitamins, amino acids, and loads of natural compounds that are essential for good health. You can break off a small portion the size of a match head and mix it in with warm milk or water to drink.

If you can find shilajit, the purest quality freezes in cold weather and turns oozy when it is warm. You can test the quality by burning a small portion. If it expands and grows into ashy bubbles, it is pure.

General: Other herbs that help heal and balance the root chakra are cloves, dandelion, horseradish, and pepper. Root vegetables, such as potatoes and carrots, also support the root chakra. As these vegetables grow underground, they have a grounded, earthy energy that resonates with the root chakra.

Herbs for the Sacral Chakra

Ayurveda: A well-known aphrodisiac, ashwagandha (meaning, literally, "horse smell") has a reputation as "Indian Viagra," but it has a lot more tricks up its sleeve than regulating sex drive. Ashwagandha is a root that is usually ground up and taken in capsule form. It increases your overall energy level—including, yes, your libido—but it also boosts the immune system and helps regulate mood. Specifically, it stabilizes serotonin levels, bringing them down if they are too high and raising them if they are too low.

General: Calendula is an herb that helps to heal the sacral chakra and promote creativity. Other beneficial herbs are sandalwood, coriander, fennel, gardenia, cinnamon, and vanilla. Foods that support healthy functioning of the chakra include meat, eggs, beans, and nuts.

Herbs for the Navel Chakra

Ayurveda: Turmeric is a standard item in any Indian kitchen, but it is also an excellent home remedy and Ayurvedic medicine in its own right. The navel chakra, Manipura, is connected to willpower, and even the digestive fire. Turmeric promotes healthy digestion by soothing or stimulating the digestive fire of the navel chakra as needed. It also helps reduce depression, which can dampen your willpower.

Turmeric often comes in powdered form. You can mix it with water and drink. A tablespoon of turmeric twice daily promotes proper digestion. Some even swear it cures the symptoms of depression.

General: Mint, jasmine, lavender, rose, basil, and ginger all help to heal the navel chakra. Pine pollen is also a potent healing agent for the navel chakra. It is full of DHEA, a substance that the body produces naturally. It enhances the adrenal glands and the endocrine system. It promotes self-confidence and willpower. It also improves digestion.

Herbs for the Heart Chakra

Ayurveda: We already mentioned ashwagandha as an herb to heal the sacral chakra. Well, it is also beneficial for the heart chakra. Another herb that soothes and heals the heart chakra is Shatavari. Shatavari is a general health tonic, which is also used correctly to support the female reproductive system. Here we are more concerned with how it encourages healthy functioning of the heart and supports the activity of the heart chakra.

It can be taken as a powder, in capsule form, or as a liquid. If you make it in powdered form, you can mix it with clarified butter. In that case, it is helpful to heat it in clarified butter to help release its healing properties.

General: Hawthorn berry, rose, and thyme all help to heal the heart chakra. Hawthorn berry especially has healing properties for the heart and helps treat heart problems such as arrhythmia and blood pressure. It is also a powerful antioxidant. It reduces stress and anxiety and promotes an emotional feeling of wellbeing and love.

Herbs for the Throat Chakra

Ayurveda: The throat chakra or vishuddha is connected with the thyroid gland. Any herbs that are used to treat thyroid disorders are also helpful for healing the throat chakra. The ayurvedic formula kanchanara guggulu is a potent remedy for problems with the thyroid gland. It removes stagnant phlegm from the body's tissues.

Also resonant with the throat chakra is brahmi. Brahmi is an herb that promotes concentration and cognitive functioning in general, and specific speech and language. It is an excellent remedy for problems afflicting the throat chakra.

General: Peppermint, salt, and lemongrass are excellent herbs for treating throat chakra problems. Slippery elm can also be used to treat inflammations and irritations of the throat. Essential for thyroid health is a sufficient level of iodine in the body. Seaweed is full of iodine, as well as many other nutrients that are often lacking in modern diets.

Herbs for the Third Eye Chakra

Ayurveda: The third eye chakra is connected to the pineal gland and the higher functions of the brain. Gotu kola is a powerful ayurvedic herb for healing and enhancing this chakra. It increases oxygen uptake in the body's cells, and accurately and most importantly in the brain. It also thickens the corpus callosum, or tissue that connects the left and right hemispheres of the brain. This increases communication between the regions and brings about the integration of intuitive and rational, holistic and linear styles of thinking. It also brings the right and left channels—Ida and Pingala—into harmony.

Meditators especially benefit from the use of this herb. It has been shown to increase intelligence in the long term.

General: In addition to eyebright, mugwort, poppy, rosemary, and lavender, passionflower is used to heal ailments of the third eye chakra. It treats insomnia, depression, anxiety, and headache, and improves mental clarity and cognition.

Herbs for the Crown Chakra

Ayurveda: The crown chakra is more rarefied and abstract than the other chakras. It is part of the subtle body system, but it is above and outside of the body. It acts as a gateway between the embodied and spiritual planes of our existence. So it needs an herb with a more subtle action.

Brahmi, mentioned earlier, in general, promotes intelligence (and even hair growth) and works to heal the crown chakra. Gotu kola also works to improve this pure chakra. Both of these herbs aid focus and clarity, which allows you to ascend to higher levels in meditation.

There is also shankhpushpi. It reduces stress and keeps the mind in a relaxed, calm, focused state. It improves memory and promotes better sleep. In general, it induces a sense of peace and spiritual wellbeing.

General: Smudging herbs such as sage help cleanse the energy in the crown chakra, which facilitates better communication between the physical and spiritual parts of our being. Sage, in particular, has been shown to increase perceptual clarity, memory, healthy brain function, and intelligence.

Also helpful is lavender, which increases clarity, reduces anxiety, soothes the nervous system, and lowers depression. It also contains some antioxidant compounds.

Essential Oils for Chakras

Aromatherapy is the use of essential oils for healing. The oils are usually massaged into the skin but can be taken orally only under the direction of a qualified specialist or doctor.

The essential oils are obtained from the roots, seeds, leaves, and berries of plants or flowers. Each has its specific ingredient that can be used for healing on many different levels.

The use of essential oils for healing is not a new concept. There is evidence dating as far back as six thousand years ago that the Chinese, Indians, and Egyptians used them for healing, cosmetics, and certain rituals or ceremonies.

In more recent times, Rene Maurice Gattefosse, a French chemist, discovered that after burning his hand and applying lavender to it, his burn healed quickly and easily. He later went on to recommend lavender to treat the wounds and gangrene suffered by soldiers in WWI.

How Does Aromatherapy Work?

Our sense of smell stimulates emotions in us. Just think about it for a moment. If you recognize a scent that was familiar to you as a child and it brought back happy positive memories, you will feel the same emotions that you felt when you were younger. Similarly, if a particular smell or fragrance is associated with bad memories, then you will experience negative feelings. When we smell something our sense of smell communicates with the amygdala and the hippocampus in the brain. This is where our emotions and our memories are stored, and we react accordingly. Another view of how essential oils work is that the molecules in the blood from the essential oils react with hormones and enzymes and this, in turn, creates an emotional reaction.

Aromatherapy is said to be beneficial to many ethical problems including anxiety, pain, constipation, psoriasis, pre-menstrual tension, rheumatoid arthritis and many others.

Aromatherapy can help to correct an imbalance in the chakras. Below I have given two examples of oils for each of the chakras to help you get started along with some of their properties. There are, of course, many others that can also be used. Please note that it is wise to seek the opinion of a suitably qualified aromatherapist before using any essential oils. It is especially important to do this if you have a diagnosed medical condition, suspect that you have, or if you are pregnant.

Root Chakra

Black Pepper—aids circulation and helps aching muscles.

Cedarwood—this oil acts as an antiseptic and aids healing.

Sacral Chakra

Clary Sage—good for menstrual problems and helps reduce infection.

Neroli—this is an excellent anti-depressant and acts as an excellent tonic.

Solar Plexus Chakra

Basil—ideal for the nervous system.

Mandarin—good for reducing stress and anxiety.

Heart Chakra

Rose—induces feelings of calmness.

Frankincense—helps emotional problems and helps to reduce stress.

Throat Chakra

Chamomile—soothing and calming

Sandalwood—acts as an antiseptic and an anti-inflammatory.

Third Eye or Brow Chakra

Hyacinth—aids emotional wellbeing.

Angelica Seed—aids in problem-solving and inward focus.

Crown Chakra

Vetiver—excellent for grounding and feeling connected to the earth.

Frankincense—emotional problems and stress.

Foods that Help with Healing

Everyone knows that the foods you eat make a difference in the way you feel. All health specialists will tell you the same thing. However, did you know that certain foods can help to heal your chakras? They can, and it is worthwhile knowing the right kinds of foods to eat. You should also be aware that drinking sufficient water is also essential. Be mindful when you eat; chewing your food and enjoying all the tastes and textures, instead of eating on the go. Your digestive tract is the most significant part of your body, and if you do not give it the respect that it needs, it can give you problems—both physical and psychological. Thus, the chakras will be affected. Take your time and get used to using all of your senses actually to get more from your food. Start thinking of your diet as being your friend, rather than merely the fuel you need to keep on living. There is a difference between just living and optimizing your health and happiness.

You have probably heard in recent health articles about the benefits of eating brightly colored vegetables. That is certainly true when it comes to chakra healing. If you can incorporate red foods and beets into your diet, you will benefit, though do not overdo the beets as this may affect your throat chakra temporarily, taken in excess. Your root chakra is keen on spiced food, and a little Tabasco sauce will not go amiss. You may even feel like your body craves this kind of taste. Learn to listen to it. It will serve you well to do so. You will also find that your root chakra enjoys lean meat, while your throat chakra is well served by a variety of fresh fruit or fruit juices. If you tend to be overweight and suffer from diabetes, avoid orange juice, as this concentration of fruit sugar may be detrimental to your health and fresh fruit would be a better option.

Your solar plexus chakra will find its healing source in whole wheat bread, which will help in digestion. Healing can also be found in teas that are intended to calm the stomach, such as peppermint and chamomile. You may see that you enjoy eating peppermints, and rather than add the unnecessary sugar to your diet, a glass of peppermint tea is the preferred option. If you do not like drinking water, why not try adding a peppermint cordial to it, as this will also help you considerably.

Green tea is the tea of choice for the heart chakra, and this is particularly good for many health issues, so you will not be doing yourself a disservice introducing it as a regular drink to take the place of coffee or soda. Coffee and tea are stimulants and if you can cut down on the amount of them you drink, the better you will feel for it. The crown chakra is not a chakra that is affected by the foods that you eat. This chakra prefers to have regular sunshine, relaxation, peace, and quiet. Meditation or relaxation exercises calm this chakra.

As a human being, you will be all too aware of your shortcomings when it comes to eating and drinking the right items. You know from general health issues how food affects the way that you feel, but did you know how vital water is to the body? Water helps to digest your food correctly, but it does much more than that. Water replenishes the body and the lost fluids that are needed for your movement and digestion. Water is especially important for those who suffer from ailments such as fibromyalgia or arthritic conditions that often forget that lack of progress and lack of water can make their situations worse. Make sure that you drink small amounts during the day, which will help your chakras and will also help you to feel better.

If you know that you have been eating in excess and that this includes all of the wrong foods, one thing that can help you to detox is nettle tea. This is a beautiful way to make sure that your body keeps up its power to clean out all of the toxins that life has let get in the way.

There are many ways that you can work on the diet that you are taking in. Most Americans are on a menu that is not all that healthy or good for them. They are used to going out to eat all of the time, picking up something that is quick and easy at a local restaurant and using that to feed their families. And when they are at home, they often do not want to spend so much time making a meal so they will make up something from the freezer section at the store. This can cause a lot of bad stuff to happen to the body because all those bad nutrients, such as the sodium, the sugar, the bad fats, and the processed carbs, are all going to wreak some havoc on the body. If the body is not able to get some of the nutrition that it needs, it is tough for the chakras to work correctly.

This means that it is time to work on making some changes to the diet that you are eating. If the description above seemed to fit into the lifestyle that you currently have, it is essential to make the changes. The first change to make is to get rid of the stuff that is so bad for the body. This includes the processed foods, such as anything that you would find at a local fast food restaurant or in the boxed and freezer section at your local store. These are so unhealthy for the whole body and are just making you sick with all the added bad nutrients and calories.

Besides, you need to be careful about the bad sugars and sodium that are in your foods, as well as the fats and the carbs that you are taking in. Sometimes these are going to sneak their way into your diet, so you need to become good at reading the labels before you purchase or make the meals for your family to eat. Watch out for some bread, some sauces, all baked goods, ice creams, French fries and more if you want to get rid of some of the wrong foods that are in your diet.

Now it is time to move on to some of the foods that you should be eating to stay healthy. Here, you want to pick out foods that are healthy and whole. These are the foods that are so good for the body because they can provide the body with all the proper nutrients that it needs, without having to put on all of the foods that are bad on the body and can make it sick. There are a few selections that you can go with including the following.

Lean meats

You will want to focus on the lean meats because they provide the body with some healthy protein that is so good for you and for helping your muscles to grow as strong as they need. While ground beef can work sometimes, but you will want to be careful because it can contain some more bad fats and cholesterol than your body needs. Lean meats like turkey, chicken, and fish are high because they provide all of the protein that the body needs without the bad stuff.

Healthy fruits and vegetables

Make sure to add as many of these to your diet as you can each day. Fresh fruits and vegetables are so good for the body because they do not contain like any of the bad stuff that you need to worry about, they are low in calories, and you will be able to get a ton of the nutrients that you are looking for to keep the body beautiful and healthy.

Healthy carbs

You do not have to avoid carbs altogether, but you do need to be careful about the types of carbs that you are consuming. You do not want to focus on the processed and white carbs, such as those found in cheap bread or those in baked goods. These are going to be turned into sugars in the body that can raise your blood sugar levels and much more. Make sure that you stick with the varieties that are whole grain and will provide some added fiber and other nutrients to the diet you consume.

Low-fat dairy

Dairy is sometimes given a bad name, but it has a lot of the calcium that you need to keep the body beautiful and healthy. This calcium, as well as vitamin D, can be high for the brain, the muscles, and so much more. You do need to be careful about the types of dairy that you consume. For example, if you have yogurt, you should make sure that you stick with low-fat plain yogurt and then add in fresh fruit if you would like to have that added flavor in there rather than going for the yogurt that already has the fruit inside.

In addition to making sure that you are eating the foods that you should, you will want to make sure that you are adequately preparing the food. You should be making these meals at home, and use approved cooking methods, such as baking and steaming, rather than frying. If you are someone who is always busy and on the run, you may want to consider working with some freezer meals. With a freezer meal, you would spend a day or two putting together some snacks and then they are ready in the freezer for you any time that you need. They do take a bit of prep work to get all put together, but the convenience of being able to grab a meal when you need it rather than wasting money and harming your body is so worth it.

When you can follow some of the tips above about dieting and eating a diet that is full of the healthy nutrients that you need to function and feel good, you are going to notice some considerable changes in your chakras. Your body will feel good, so your chakras can perform the way that they should. Give it a try and dedicate yourself to eating foods that are healthier than ever, and you are sure to notice that your chakras will feel better in no time as well.

Root Chakra

The root chakra's element is Earth so adding root vegetables that grow deep within the earth to your diet can help you strengthen your connection to the physical world.

- Red colored foods: red apples, watermelon, and pomegranates
- Hot spices: red cayenne peppers, paprika, and horseradish
- Vegetables from the ground: potatoes, beets, and carrots; garlic, ginger, and onions
- Animal proteins: red meat and eggs
- Red herbal teas such as rooibos or hibiscus

If you are a vegetarian, red beans and lentils are great for your root chakra.

Sacral Chakra

In the second chakra, you move from standing on the solid ground of the root chakra to the fluid world of sacral chakra. In the body, these fluids are the essences of life such as blood, tears, and lymph. Water is the critical element of life on earth. Root chakra helps to keep us grounded, the sacral chakra help to flow our creativity.

- Orange colored foods: oranges, tangerines, and mangos
- Carrots, pumpkins, melons, and nuts
- This chakra's element is water, stay hydrated and drink plenty of water, coconut water, or herbal teas
- Spices: cinnamon, sesame seeds, and vanilla

Solar Plexus Chakra

With this chakra, we should feed it with foods that help transform the energy from our first two chakras and send it to the heart chakra. Yellow is a natural mood enhancer.

- Yellow colored foods: corn, fresh pineapple, lemons, and bananas
- Grains and fiber: granola, brown rice, and whole wheat bread
- Digestive-friendly foods: kefir, kombucha, and yogurt
- Seeds: flax and sunflower
- Teas: peppermint, ginger, and chamomile

Heart Chakra

This chakra is the bridge between our three lower and three upper chakras. It is all about balance within ourselves, our relationships, and whatever is happening in our environment.

- Leafy vegetables: lettuce, broccoli, spinach
- Green fruits: limes, green apples, and avocados
- Green beans: lima beans and mung beans
- Green tea
- Spices: basil, thyme, and cilantro

Throat Chakra

This chakra—the first of the spiritual chakras—represents willpower and responsibility. Throat chakra blockage can manifest as a cold or a sore throat or headaches. Trying to speak our truths is the best food that we can feed our throat chakra.

- Liquids: water, fresh juices (with no added sugar), and herbal teas
- Blue foods: blueberries, figs, and kelp
- Fruits grow on trees: apples, pears, and plums

- All types of fruits
- Spices: salt, lemon grass

Third Eye Chakra

Since this chakra is located in our head rather than in our torsos like the first five chakras, it has a little different nature.

- Purple-colored fruits: eggplant, concord grapes, and blackberries
- Metal detoxers from the ground like mushrooms
- Nuts, seeds, and legumes: raw walnuts, sprouted almonds, and poppy seeds
- Chocolate
- Liquids: red wines and grape juice
- Spices: lavender, poppy seed, and mugwort

Crown Chakra

Since this chakra represents our spiritual connection to the universe, it does not benefit from healing foods. It is more likely to benefit from spending time in nature, being in direct sunlight, and drinking water.

Fasting and detoxifying can be beautiful ways to recharge our crown chakra. Detoxing can help our bodies flush out toxins, boost our energy, and clear our mind.

Purified or salt water absorbed through the skin or top of head or scalp; aloe vera; seeds like chia and sesame; bone and vegetable broths; extremely light foods like mushrooms, garlic, ginger, onion, coconut, lychee and other tropical fruits can also be used to strengthen crown chakra.

Affirmations

Affirmations are anything that we think or say. Using the power of affirmations is one of the most effective ways to balance our chakras and heal ourselves. Our thoughts create our reality, and that is why practicing positive affirmations can create positive changes in our body, mind, and soul.

When practicing affirmations, sit or lie down in a quiet place and focus on the location of each chakra. Say out loud in a confident voice or silently meditate on each affirmation. Visualize a wheel spinning face-up in a clockwise direction in the specific color frequency of each chakra.

Root Chakra

- *I nourish and nurture myself, and I have a right to be here*
- *I am safe, peaceful and protected*
- *I am grounded, stable, connected to the earth and open to the positive energy that flows through me*

Sacral Chakra

- *I embrace my sexuality and sensuality*
- *I nurture myself*
- *I use my creativity for the higher purpose*
- *I am kind and compassionate*
- *I feel passionate about my life and am confident in who I am.*

Solar Plexus Chakra

- *I honor myself, be who I am in the world, and express that power without fear*
- *I am positively empowered and successful in all my ventures*
- *My body is strong and healthy*
- *I take responsibility for my life*
- *I can do anything I set my mind to, and I am worthy of all that the Universe has to offer*

Heart Chakra

- *I feel my true feelings, desires, and passions and be at home in my heart*

- *I open myself to deep self-love*
- *I open myself to healthy and nurturing relationships*
- *I am very grateful for all that I have and forgive myself and others*
- *I love my life and have compassion for all of the people in it*

Throat Chakra

- *I express myself truthfully and trust the Universe to bless this energy center for the good*
- *I speak my truth, and I have a balance between heart and mind*
- *I think before I talk and can say "no" when I need to*
- *I love myself, and I express my love for others*

Third Eye Chakra

- *I use my intuition wisely*
- *I have a sense of knowing everything I need to know*
- *All that I need is within me*
- *I learn from the challenges in my life and trust what I see*
- *I open myself to insights, clarity, and the knowledge of elders*
- *I know my life's purpose, and I am open to gaining new wisdom*

Crown Chakra

- *I have a bright and open connection with all people and all things*
- *I am one with the Divine energy, and I honor the divine in me and others*
- *I am grounded on earth, connected with heavens, and the whole of Universe*

The Manifesting Current

Once you have practiced with each chakra from root to crown, then reverse the order and move from top to root. The flow upward through your chakras is the liberating current, and it helps remove blocks. The flow downward is the manifesting current, and it helps bring the pure potentiality of the Universe into your physical form. To activate the manifesting current, you can say the following affirmations.

- Crown chakra: I AM INFINITY.
- Third eye chakra: I AM DEEP PERCEPTION.
- Throat chakra: I AM TRUTH.
- Heart chakra: I AM LOVE.
- Solar plexus chakra: I AM POWER.
- Sacral chakra: I AM PLEASURE.
- Root chakra: I AM SACRED GROUND.
  You can finish with something like:
- *I have support from below*
- *I am active from above*
- *I radiate power*
- *I receive love*
- *I am wealthy*
- *I am joyful*
- *I am healthy*
- *I am free*

CONCLUSION

Thank you for reading this essential introduction book to chakras. Hopefully, you are now a little bit more knowledgeable on the topic and will be able to start focusing on balancing your inner chakra points.

This book contains steps and strategies on how to awaken your chakras, how to balance these energies emanating from the chakra points in your body, and how to use this knowledge to make your life better.

This book will teach you exactly that. This guide contains all the things that you need to know about chakras—the chakra points, the strengths and weaknesses of each location, the colors, notes and gemstones that you can equip yourself with and, more importantly, how to awaken and balance your chakras so that one end is not overpowered by the other. Learn real stuff from this book and see how you can manifest and radiate positive energy through your chakras.

Thanks again for reading this book! I hope you enjoy it!